Clickable Nonprofit Blog Posts

The Complete Nonprofit Guide to Blog Post Strategy & Messaging Plus 54 Nonprofit Blog Article Ideas!

The Nonprofit Marketing Series

Rob Ainbinder & Nikki Corbett

Copyright © 2021 Rob Ainbinder & Nikki Corbett
All rights reserved.

DEDICATION

This book is dedicated to the nonprofit marketing managers and marketing coordinators who work tirelessly in order to provide services to those in need in their community. We hope this book gives you some inspiration to write amazing blog posts to capture more donations, volunteers and the public's attention.

CONTENTS

ACKNOWLEDGMENTS   5

1. CAPTURE YOUR AUDIENCE WITH VOICE AND TONE   6
    Why Voice and Tone Are Important   6
    Who Is Your Target Audience?   6
    The Difference Between Voice and Tone   7
    How to Find Your Organization's Voice   8
    Put Your Brand Standards in Writing   9

2. HOW TO CRAFT YOUR MARKETING MESSAGE   10
    What Is a Marketing Message? And Why Is It Important?   10
    3 Steps to Crafting Your Message   10

3. SEARCH ENGINE OPTIMIZATION FOR YOUR BLOG POST   13
    The Nuts and Bolts of SEO   14
    And a Few Technicalities…   15
    Summary–Where to Use SEO Keyword(s) or Key Phrase(s) in Blog Posts   17

4. BLOG POST TITLES   18
    Headline Formulas Work   18
    Use Keywords   19
    Getting Down to Logistics   19

5. BLOG POST STRUCTURE   23
    Introduction   23
    The Main Body: Structure and Features   23
    Mid-Post Call to Action   24
    Conclusion and Call to Action   24

Clickable Nonprofit Blog Posts

6. 54 BLOG POST IDEAS	**26**
7. RESOURCES	**30**
Websites	30
Chrome Browser Plug-ins	30
ABOUT THE AUTHORS	**31**

ACKNOWLEDGMENTS

Rob wants to acknowledge the nonprofits he has had the opportunity to serve, including Geek Club Books, Second Harvest FoodBank of Northwest North Carolina, Junior Achievement of the Triad, SECU House, and Triad Highland Games. They are the reason for this book series. Rob also wants to thank his co-author, Nikki, for graciously contributing to the book series.

Nikki would like to acknowledge the nonprofits she has had the opportunity to serve, including The Downtown Greenway (Greensboro, NC), Samaritan Maids, the Time to Shine Scholarship for Women, and the HUGS Foundation, as well as her many clients that support nonprofits through their own efforts.. It is her goal to help make the world a better place, one communication at a time.

1. CAPTURE YOUR AUDIENCE WITH VOICE AND TONE

Whether you are writing a blog article, social media post, website copy, a letter, or e-newsletter, it's essential to use the right language to get your message across. If you want your writing to evoke a certain response—from the public, from donors, or from volunteers—you'll need to think about your audience first. And, you need to speak their language.

Why Voice and Tone Are Important

In essence, your brand voice is what you say in your communications—all communications. And your tone is how you say it. Each company has a unique brand voice and tone—and nonprofit organizations are no different. The way you communicate is one of the ways that sets you apart from other nonprofits.

Your brand's voice and tone should help attract the right audience, but without detracting from your message. Your voice and tone will also help develop relationships over time. Here are a few things you'll need to consider when determining your organization's voice and tone.

- Determine what your target audience needs.
- Know where the content will be used.
- Decide what you want to say and how you want to say it.
- Put your brand standards in writing.

Who Is Your Target Audience?

As a nonprofit, you may have different audiences to appeal to: donors, board members, grantmakers, foundations, volunteers, staff members, the general public, etc. While your voice will always remain consistent, you may need to change your tone slightly in order to appeal to your target audience.

So, what does your target audience want to hear? Do you need to speak casually, or do you need to provide more technical information? Your voice and tone need to resonate with each intended audience. The wrong brand tone will be perceived as awkward, tacky, or inauthentic. The right tone will be comfortable, appropriate, and engaging. And if your voice and tone are off target, your entire message will get lost—and forgotten.

The first step is to put yourself in your audience's shoes and ask the following questions.

- What does this organization mean to them?
- How do we make their lives better?
- What is important—and not important—to them?
- How do we help solve a problem or concern that they care about?

The Difference Between Voice and Tone

Your nonprofit's voice is both what you say and how you say it; in essence, it's your culture. Your tone is how you adjust your voice for each platform in order to relay your message properly. Your voice can include specific vocabulary, as well as optics and visuals used to convey or enhance your values, vision, and message.

Your brand tone is how you approach communication. Is your nonprofit serious or happy-go-lucky? Does your vision and mission appeal to youth or seniors? Your tone consists of the cadence and even specific words you use to communicate your message and emotion. And your tone is the language your audience already uses.

So, at this point, you're probably wondering, How do we find our voice? Let's take a look at that…

How to Find Your Organization's Voice

Finding your voice may seem daunting, but it's really easier than you think. We recommend taking the following three steps to determine your organization's voice.

1. **Define your prime value(s).** If you haven't created your vision, mission, and culture statements, this is probably the time to do so. Your mission is what you do; your vision is the ideal future of your business; and your culture is how you behave. Once you've defined your values, or what drives your organization, you can determine the words, phrases, and approaches to help underline your intent.

2. **Start with your tagline.** A company tagline is another essential tool that lets your audience know what you are all about—in just a phrase or sentence. Your tagine should resonate with your intended audience, and you should use it everywhere you can. An established tagline can help guide you toward your brand voice.

3. **Test and measure your communication.** Before going full speed ahead, you may want to test your voice and tone—or more than one approach—with different audience samples. Also called A/B Testing, it's a perfect way to practice broadcasting your message among smaller segments of your audience to determine the winning voice/tone that best resonates with your target audience.

Put Your Brand Standards in Writing

The voice and tone you use will define your nonprofit organization. Once you've determined your brand voice and tone, along with any other standards of written and/or verbal communication, it's essential to put those standards in writing. It's what's called a Brand Style Guide.

Documenting your brand standards in writing ensures that no matter who is communicating on behalf of your organization—an internal staff member or an external contractor—the voice and tone are always consistent. You can even be specific about preferred terminology to use as well as particular words and phrases to avoid.

The most important factor to note is that your brand's voice should always be consistent. If your organization deals with serious matters, then your social media posts should use that same voice. For example, it would feel out of place for an organization that helps fight world hunger to post a humorous social media meme about where someone's next meal is coming from.

Finally, perfecting your organization's voice and tone may be an ongoing effort. And it may also evolve over time. Think about big brands like Coke, Pepsi, Levi's, Johnson & Johnson, etc. Their messaging has changed over the decades, and you may find your nonprofit's messaging evolve as well.

2. HOW TO CRAFT YOUR MARKETING MESSAGE

What you say and how you say it is always important—no matter your goal or what your organization represents. Using the right words can make the difference between receiving the donations to reach your fundraising goal or falling short of that goal. So, the best way to appeal to your target audience is to communicate with them on as personal a level as possible. (Refer back to Chapter 1 on Voice and Tone.)

What Is a Marketing Message? And Why Is It Important?

Your marketing message entails what you tell your audience about who you are and what you do, so that they'll take the precise action you'd like them to take. What you say has the power to influence one way or the other. That's why it's essential to craft your marketing message in the right way.

The purpose of your marketing message is to develop a deep connection and elicit either an emotional or logical response. You want your audience to feel like you're speaking just to them. In essence, you want to create a group of insiders, including skeptic outsiders, that grows into a tribe of fervent supporters.

3 Steps to Crafting Your Message

1. **Define Your Target Market**
   The purpose of any communication is to hook your audience so they want more. So, before you write a single word, you need to know whom you are speaking to.

   In recent years, many companies have created buyer personas for their product(s) and/or service(s)—even going so far as to give each persona a name (Phoebe Philanthropist, Sam Soccer Dad, Brenda Busy Business

Owner, etc.).

Here's how you define your target market...

2. **Identify Pain Points**
   What are your clients'/funders'/donors' frustrations and fears? And also, what are their dreams, hopes, and desires? What is their 'problem,' and how do you solve it? How will volunteering, donating, or otherwise becoming involved with your organization make them happier?

   Once you identify these critical factors, you can find a way to speak to these issues while presenting your organization and its individual and/or community benefits. In fact, through this process, you answer your own Why.

3. **Provide Your Benefits-Driven Solution**
   Now it's time to take a deep dive into your blog article and show your audience just how great you are—and why you're important to them. Show that you understand them and truly care about their needs, wants, and desires as well as their hopes, fears, and frustrations. To do this, you have to provide an answer to this question: What's in it for me? (WIIFM)

   It's not about you! While you have permission to talk about how great you are, it's vital not to make your message about you. Your message is always about your audience. One way to help you avoid making your communication about you is to avoid the use of *I*, *we*, *us*, and *our* as much as possible. Instead, use *you*, *your*, and *yours* more often.

   You're selling a feeling. Mix emotions and logic in your writing. Emotions prompt action, while logic underlines why that action makes sense. Every decision we make is emotion-based... whether it's donating to a nonprofit, selecting a university, or simply buying a toaster. You're **never** 'selling' the opportunity to donate to your cause.

However, you are *always* selling how a person will *feel* when they're making a donation—and how they'll *feel* after the donation.

Help people connect. As human beings, we all want connection. We want to feel like we are part of a group. So, it's important to help people see themselves in others. By drawing a parallel with people just like them, they'll learn how they can benefit from the action you now want more people to take. However, you'll need to go a little further than providing a simple testimonial or review. Helping people feel like they belong is the true power behind your messaging.

Differentiate your organization. You may not be the only nonprofit in your space in your specific region. For example, there may very well be other good organizations working to eliminate hunger, homelessness, and discrimination. So, the best way to differentiate is to highlight how you are different. Why is your organization unique and exciting? And what does your audience get by working with you that they won't get elsewhere? And how can you personalize their experience?

With these methods, you can craft an enticing message that will help your organization stand out and achieve the goals you are reaching for. Then you'll be ready to set higher goals the next time!

3. SEARCH ENGINE OPTIMIZATION FOR YOUR BLOG POST

In Chapter 1, we discussed capturing voice and tone. But if you want your posts to be found organically online (without putting advertising dollars behind it), then almost none of this book matters if you don't use Search Engine Optimization (SEO).

Why SEO?

For search engines like Google® and Bing® to rank your blog article and show it in search engine results, you need to be search engine friendly in what you post to your website and blog. Otherwise, you don't stand a chance of someone stumbling upon your blog article unless they are already on your website. The good news is that you can use SEO so that search engines can crawl your blog article, make a copy of it to show searchers, and understand what it's about. And, more importantly, you can make it an enjoyable read for your visitors too.

It All Starts with Keyword Research

SEO-optimized posts utilize one or more related keywords and/or keyword phrases. So, your first step is to perform some keyword research to discover how to best promote your organization.

Keyword research involves a lot more than just typing some search terms into your computer to see what results you get. We highly encourage you to find a reputable digital marketer (local or anywhere in your country) to assist with this process.

In fact, a solid digital marketer will be able to use a variety of tools to determine the right keywords and phrases that you can use in your region. Of course, you could access the same tools—for fees that add up quickly—but still not know the best way to go about managing the keyword research process. So, it's often better to pay a professional to get the best results while you focus on other things in your nonprofit.

Determining Your Keywords/Longtail Phrases

First, you'll want to provide your digital marketer with a list of keywords and longtail phrases (2–5 words) that make sense for your nonprofit. You'll also want to provide a list of your direct and/or indirect competitors. Their next step is to flesh out your provided list of search terms and add to it in order to find the terms that will work best for you. From their work, you should receive key terms and phrases in these categories:

- High- to low-volume searches and…
- Low- to medium-volume competition.

It's the sweet spot—and it's different for every nonprofit. Ultimately, you don't want to waste your time ranking for keywords and phrases that either no one is searching for or that have been commandeered by bigger nonprofits, making it not worth your time or money. An expert digital marketer will also dig into what your competitors are doing to determine where best to position your organization's brand. The bottom line is that your professional digital marketer will help you find the most sensible way to use your marketing budget.

The Nuts and Bolts of SEO

Now that we know what SEO is and why it's important, let's look at the SEO elements that need to be included in each blog article (and each website page for that matter).

Articles that use the best SEO use their primary keywords/phrases in the following places, while using supplementary/secondary keywords and phrases in other places. It's essential to use your designated primary keyword in the following places.

>**Blog Title:** Use your keyword or phrase as early as possible in your article headline.

>**First Paragraph:** Use your keyword or longtail phrase in

the first paragraph, or at least within the first 100 words of your article.

Subheadings: Be sure to use your primary keyword or phrase in at least one subheading.

In Text: Make use of your keyword or longtail phrase *a few times* throughout the text of your article.

Calls to Action (CTAs): Use your keyword or phrase in one Call to Action. (See Chapter 7.)

NOTE: Refrain from what's called keyword stuffing—overuse of your keyword or phrase throughout your article. Only use your keyword where it feels and sounds natural. You don't want to turn your reader off. But more importantly, you don't want search engines to flag your content for being "spammy." Also, avoid anything like "hidden" keywords. Using hidden keywords is a technique where extra keywords are typed onto your website page, then the font color is changed to match the background color; thus, making them invisible to site visitors—but highly visible to bots, crawlers, and search engines. These tactics will get your website flagged or even banned by search engines.

And a Few Technicalities...

Finally, you need to give the search engines a little more information. Specifically, you'll also need to use your primary key phrase in a few 'technical' areas. Provide this information to your web developer, or the person on your marketing team who is posting your articles to your website, for the highest performing blog post.

URL: Your URL is your website address that appears in the search bar. It's important to also use your key phrase here (with hyphens)

Example: www.nonprofitagency.org/how-your-donation-is-used

Title Tag: Your Title Tag is the blue-lettered title to your website link that appears in search engine results. Be sure to use your keyword or phrase here. Your Title Tag should be no more than 70 characters in all, including spaces. Otherwise, your title will get cut off.

Example:
How Your Donation Is Used | Nonprofit Agency

Meta Description: The Meta Description is the text that appears underneath your Title Tag in search engine results. It's important to use your primary keyword or phrase here too. Your Meta Description should be no more than 160 characters in all, including spaces. Otherwise, your description will get cut off. Consider the Meta Description your opportunity to entice a reader, like an ad, to click through the search results and read your post. It's a summary of your post with a promotional twist.

Alt Tags: Alt Tags are used with any photos that you add to your blog post. When uploading photos to your blog article page, you will have an option to designate an Alt Tag for each photo. For the best optimization, it's also important to use your keyword or phrase as the Alt Tag for each photo on the page. Search engines will also crawl these areas of your site to help determine the quality of your blog article.

Summary—Where to Use SEO Keyword(s) or Key Phrase(s) in Blog Posts

- Blog Title
- First Paragraph/First 100 Words
- At least one Subheading (H1 and H2 Headings)
- In text (several places, including relevant variations/synonyms)

Clickable Nonprofit Blog Posts

- CTAs (Calls to Action)
- URL
- Title Tag
- Meta Description
- Alt tags

4. BLOG POST TITLES

What's in a name? Or a blog title, in this case? A lot.

A blog title is just as important as the content that goes into the blog. Think about your own time spent on social media or perusing through a website. If the title doesn't attract you, then you probably won't be enticed to read it. So, start by paying attention to the headlines that make you click and read.

Several factors play into the clickability of your blog article: title length, title content, and power words. To start, each blog article should have a purpose: educate, entertain, inform, or persuade (i.e., sell). As such, your blog article and title need to accomplish one of three overall goals in order to get people to click.

- **Make it personal.** In life, if it's not personal it doesn't matter. So, take a moment to get inside the psyche of your target audience. What's important to them?
- **Make it actionable.** What do you want the reader to do because of this article? Make it clear... don't make them guess.
- **Create curiosity.** Who doesn't love a mystery? We humans are inquisitive creatures, and we can't help but consume something that makes us curious.

Headline Formulas Work

When creating your blog title, think about answering the What's-In-It-For-Me question for your site visitor. Just as humans are curious creatures, we also tend to be predictable. That's why headline formulas still work—no matter how sophisticated we get as consumers. The most popular headlines follow the following formulas:

> Number + Adjective + Keyword + Rationale + Promise

> Example:

6 Great Nonprofit Fundraisers & Why They'll Boost Your Bottom Line

How to…

Famous comparison (e.g., *Lessons Learned from Studying Richard Branson's Early Years*)

Scarcity (*Little Known Tricks for… The Secret of…*)

Big promise (*The Best Way to… The Ultimate Guide for…*)

Negativity (*Don't Do This When… You Should Worry if…*)

Use Keywords

It's important to use your keywords or search terms in the right places if you want your article to be stumbled upon while people are surfing and searching online. Search engines need to know what your article is about in order to display it in search results. Refer back to Chapter 3 for more details.

When writing for the online world, we do recommend doing a little keyword research in advance—for your industry and your region. Then be sure to use your keyword(s) or search phrase in the headline of your article. If possible, it's also important to place your keywords closer to the beginning of your blog title.

Getting Down to Logistics

Now that you have your concept, let's start constructing. We recommend utilizing the following three tactics to make an enticing, clickable blog article headline.

1. Word Count and Character Count: If your blog title is too short, then you're probably not providing enough information about what the reader can expect to get from your article. And if the title is too long, you've probably lost their attention before they read it because they're already scrolling past.

According to expert sites like HubSpot, headlines with around six words or 55 characters (including spaces and punctuation) tend to earn the highest number of click-throughs. Of course, your titles don't need to hit these numbers exactly. But if your title falls within a reasonable range (e.g., approximately five to nine words or 45-65 characters), you'll be fine.

2. First 3 Words and Last 3 Words: Next, pay attention to the first three words and the last three words of your blog title. Since internet readers tend to visually scan their screens, you'll need to pay attention to the beginning and end of your blog title. Do these six words provide enough information so that your potential reader will understand what your article is about, what they will get from reading it, and whether that result is meaningful to them?

3. Power Words: Once you have your title ready, we recommend you take a deeper dive into your word selection. The most persuasive words in the English language are *new, free, you/your, instant(ly),* and *because*. But those aren't the only words you should focus on. The words you choose can evoke emotion, and it's those emotions—positive or negative—that cause us to take an action (in this case, click and read).

- Curiosity
- Urgency
- Confusion
- Helplessness
- Anger
- Safety
- Satisfied
- Happy
- Alive
- Inspired
- Relaxed
- Peaceful
- And more!

In addition, words can cause people to feel a state of being or desire, which can also prompt the action you want them to take. Consider this list of emotion-driven reasons to take action.

- Influence
- Community
- Exclusivity
- Fear of missing out (FOMO)
- Scarcity
- And more!

By choosing more enticing words, you'll garner additional clicks and read-through. And by examining each word critically, you'll be able to create a more powerful headline.

> Example: 7 *Reasons to Donate to a Charity This Year* might sound better as 7 *Big Reasons to Donate to Your Favorite Charity This Year.*

By incorporating the words *big* and *your favorite* to the blog title, you make it more compelling—and provide a more personal reason to click and read, then hopefully take action.

Practice makes perfect! We recommend writing several titles for each blog article. Keep playing with different words and combinations until you discover the most enticing title.

Feeling stuck? You'll find numerous sources for power words and influential words online.

BONUS TIP: When it comes to listicle-type articles, odd numbers such as the example above (7 Reasons…) tend to garner more clicks than even numbers, with the exception of 10. So, *101 Super Things We Did with Your Donation Last Year* may perform better than the same article using *100*.

Does this sound like a lot of details to think about for a simple blog article title? With a little practice—just like riding a bike—you'll be incorporating these steps without even thinking. Creating

Clickable Nonprofit Blog Posts

a catchy blog article title will become second nature before you know it!

5. BLOG POST STRUCTURE

Writing a blog is like telling a story. And just like any story, it should have a beginning, a middle, and an end. In a blog, we call these elements the introduction, main body, and conclusion/call to action. Let's take a look at these elements and what you need to know.

Introduction

Aside from the meat of your article, your introduction is one of the most important elements. Use this opening paragraph (three to five sentences) to make a connection with your reader, introduce the subject, and let the reader know why it's important to them (i.e., why they should read it).

Then you can begin writing the meat of your article. Be sure to speak in a voice that makes sense for your organization, and write in a way that is both inviting and comfortable to your reader.

The Main Body: Structure and Features

Your sentence length should be shorter rather than longer. Remember that newspapers write toward an eighth-grade audience. So, in general, you should too (unless your target market requires more complex language [e.g., scientists, PhDs, engineers, etc.]). This is essential for two reasons: 1) you never want to talk over your audience and 2) search engines determine the value of your content by calculating the reading ease.

Be sure to use subheadings throughout your article. Remember, many people will scan an article before they read it. Strategic subheadings will provide a glimpse into what each section is about. (You'll find us using this and other techniques throughout this book and the entire nonprofit series.)

In addition to shorter sentences, search engines also like to see shorter paragraphs (typically three to five sentences) and no more than three paragraphs between subheadings.

Depending on the length of your blog, you should also try to include one or more bulleted or numbered lists. A reader may choose to read the entire article or just the parts that interest them. So, providing subheadings and lists gives your reader the opportunity to visually scan your blog article and grab the information they need.

BONUS TIP: When you've finished writing your blog article, read your article title, subtitle, and subheadings. Do they make sense? Be sure that each one flows to the next and helps guide your reader through the article.

Mid-Post Call to Action

No matter how hard you work on your blog post there will be a percentage of readers that don't make it to the end of your post.

It might be that you did such a good job in the first half of your post that your reader is ready to take action.

This is why we recommend placing your call to action mid-way through the blog post.

Conclusion and Call to Action

Your last paragraph is your opportunity to summarize your article and remind your reader about why the subject at hand is important to them. In addition, when your reader reaches the end of your article, you need to answer the following question for them: What do you want me to do now?

That's why it's essential to have a clear call to action at the end of your blog article. Do you want your reader to donate to your cause, join your email list, sign up to volunteer?

Be specific about what action you'd like the reader to take after reading your article. A clear call to action will reinforce your intent and encourage readers to respond to your request.

Summary—Elements of a Blog Article

- Blog Title (use keyword/phrase, 40–69 characters)
- Blog Subheading (if appropriate)
- Text Subheadings (H1 and H2 Headings – keyword phrase used at least once, plus relevant variations/synonyms)
- First paragraphs catchy and emotionally appealing
- Bulleted/Numbered Lists
- CTA mid-blog
- CTA at end
- 2–3 Internal Links
- Links to 2 reputable industry sources
- Voice and tone match brand's editorial guidelines
- Post addresses pain points, priorities, needs

6. 54 BLOG POST IDEAS

Timely/Newsworthy Articles
- External news relevant to audience with commentary from or tie-in to organization

How-To Articles
- Articles that use how-to guides related to your organization (For example, for a birding organization: how to make a backyard feeder, plant a bird-friendly garden, etc.)
- How to choose a nonprofit to donate to

Personal/Community Profiles
- Profiles of employees/staff, directors, donors, community partners and organizations, volunteers, board members, program participants, beneficiaries, funded researchers

Internal News/Announcements
- Interesting or press-worthy news: campaigns, events, awards, hires, organizational changes, research, volunteer opportunities, etc.
- Future fundraising goals
- New event calendar

Personal Stories
- Stakeholders, directors, community members, donation recipients, beneficiaries, etc. write a post about their experience with your organization

Q&A
- Questions you get asked a lot are perfect blog article topics!

Education/Information
- Cover topics that help the public and potential donors and partners understand who you are and what you do as part of an awareness or advocacy campaign.
- Fundraising best practices

- What you wish everyone knew

Book/Product Reviews
- Reviews about books, products, movies, services, etc. that relate to your organization

Listicles (list-style articles)
- Top ways to support your organization, and other list-type articles
- All of the ways someone can give to your organization
- Wish list of your organization's current needs
- Questions to ask before donating to a nonprofit
- How to be a better donor
- How to know if you're making a difference
- Seasonal donations needed
- Top events for the year (past or future)

BONUS Articles with odd-numbered lists tend to perform better.

Case Studies/Success Stories
- Feature your organization in action with participants, beneficiaries, sponsors, corporate/city partners, other agencies, and more.

Leadership Message
- Periodic personal message from the executive director
- Responses to published articles, findings, etc.
- What would happen if your organization disappeared tomorrow
- The right time to give
- Why your organization is different

Personal Insights
- Experience, advice, practical tips, quotes, inspiration for change, or lessons learned from a local/industry professional

Interviews
- Interview sessions with volunteers, participants, local

influencers, beneficiaries, subject matter experts, etc.

From-the-Field Updates
- News from daily work and improvements in the community
- Organizational challenges
- Real-time updates

Results/Accomplishments
- Year in Review or Year Ahead posts—written and/or visual using infographics
- Campaign milestones
- Flashback to a previous win
- The results of a big donation

Holidays & Celebration/Remembrance Days
- Tie-ins to upcoming holiday or days/weeks/months of celebration that relate to your organization or cause

Industry Trends
- Trends, hot topics, and innovations that impact your organization and daily operations
- Research study or report that impacts your organization

The Unusual
- Out-of-the-box opportunities to fundraise or call attention to your cause

Donation/Volunteer Impacts
- How a single donation or volunteer opportunity can make an impact.
- Where each dollar goes
- How people can make a difference in their everyday lives
- A donor meets a beneficiary
- Highlight different types of donors

A Day in the Life…
- Highlight a day in the life of someone in or related to your organization, a potential beneficiary, etc.

Thank You
- A thank you letter to someone who has made a difference in your organization or community, or for your cause
- Donor of the Year

Guest Blog
- Invite a community member or someone important to your organization to create a guest blog for your website.

Behind the Scenes
- The process from donation to beneficiary
- Setting up for an event/fundraiser
- Making community connections
- How your donation has been used

Resources
- Share resources (books, blogs, articles, podcasts, websites, social media accounts, etc.) for finding out more about your cause.

7. RESOURCES

Figuring out your topic can be daunting. To help your nonprofit generate topic ideas and understand some SEO, we've put together our list of favorite free tools.

Websites

Headline Analyzer - CoSchedule
https://coschedule.com/headline-analyzer

Ubersuggest - Keyword Tool
https://neilpatel.com/ubersuggest/

Answer the Public - Topic Generator
https://answerthepublic.com/

Google Trends - Keyword Trends
https://trends.google.com/trends/?geo=US

Chrome Browser Plug-ins

Ahrefs SEO Toolbar
https://chrome.google.com/webstore/detail/ahrefs-seo-toolbar/hgmoccdbjhknikckedaaebbpdeebhiei?hl=en

Keywords Everywhere
https://chrome.google.com/webstore/detail/keywords-everywhere-keywo/hbapdpeemoojbophdfndmlgdhppljgmp?hl=en

ABOUT THE AUTHORS

Rob Ainbinder is a digital marketer with more than 18 years of experience. He assists clients through his firm, Why People Click, with Google Ads and search engine optimization. In his spare time, he enjoys cooking barbecue and other foods, as well as reading and writing. During NFL football season, you can find him cheering on the New England Patriots. You can also find him at Rob Ainbinder.com

Nikki Corbett is president and owner of Precise Creative, a one-stop marketing agency providing web and blog content management, social media management, marketing, strategy, graphic design, and more. Nikki enjoys spending time on and around the water by boat, paddleboard, kayak, and surfboard. You'll also find her reading and writing in her spare time, as well as running a North Carolina travel blog, Portable NC.

Printed in Great Britain
by Amazon